TRANSITIONING INTO SENIOR HIGH SCHOOL

YOUR PASSPORT TO SUCCESS IN SENIOR HIGH SCHOOL

C.D. Minnis B.Sc., M.Ed.

Copyright © 2017 Carol D. Minnis

All rights reserved. In accordance with U.S. Copyright Act of 1976, the scanning, uploading, and electronic sharing of any part of this book without permission of the publisher constitute unlawful piracy and theft of the author's intellectual property. No part of this book may be reproduced in any form by any electronic or mechanical means (including photocopying, recording or information storage and retrieval) without permission in writing from the author or publisher. Thank you for your support of the author's rights.

Published by Richter Publishing LLC www.richterpublishing.com

ISBN:1945812095

ISBN-13:9781945812095

DISCLAIMER

This book is designed to provide information on education only. This information is provided and sold with the knowledge that the publisher and author do not offer any legal or medical advice. In the case of a need for any such expertise consult with the appropriate professional. This book does not contain all information available on the subject. This book has not been created to be specific to any individual people or organization's situation or needs. Reasonable efforts have been made to make this book as accurate as possible. However, there may be typographical and or content errors. Therefore, this book should serve only as a general guide. This book contains information that might be dated or erroneous and is intended only to educate and entertain. The author and publisher shall have no liability or responsibility to any person or entity regarding any loss or damage incurred, or alleged to have incurred, directly or indirectly, by the information contained in this book or as a result of anyone acting or failing to act upon the information in this book. You hereby agree never to sue and to hold the author and publisher harmless from any and all claims arising out of the information contained in this book. You hereby agree to be bound by this disclaimer, covenant not to sue and release. You may return this book within the guaranteed time period for a full refund. In the interest of full disclosure, this book contains affiliate links that might pay the author or publisher a commission upon any purchase from the company. While the author and publisher take no responsibility for any virus or technical issues that could be caused by such links, the business practices of these companies and or the performance of any product or service, the author or publisher has used the product or service and makes a recommendation in good faith based on that experience. All characters appearing in this work have given permission for their photos to be published. Any resemblance to real persons, living or dead, is purely coincidental. The opinions and stories in this book are the views of the author and not that of the publisher.

DEDICATED TO OUR MOTHER
EVELYN GERTRUDE TAYLOR-MINNIS
NOVEMBER 15TH, 1935- NOVEMBER 20TH, 2016

You were the best woman any child could have had for a mother. We were blessed to be raised by you. Your selflessness was remarkable. Not only did you make us, your children, feel loved, but you had a gift of making each person you came into contact with feel special. To know you, was to love you.

Thank you for teaching us how to be respectful, honest, obedient, generous and resilient. More importantly, thank you for teaching us to fear God and walk in His ways.

ACKNOWLEDGEMENTS

Editors: Mrs. Suzanne Knowles – Ministry of Education
Mrs. Dellie Robinson-Thompson – Language Arts Teacher, Government High School
Ms. Joan Norman – Former Language Arts Department Head, St. Anne's School
Mrs. Barbara Petersen – Professional Proofreading Services, New Jersey, USA

Mrs. Eulease Beneby – Superintendent, Southeastern District & Former Principal of C.V. Bethel Senior High School
Mrs. Josephine Parker – Former Principal, C.V. Bethel Senior High School
Ms. Princess Fawkes – Principal, C.V. Bethel Senior High School
Mr. Herbert Oembler – Principal, C.I. Gibson Senior High School

Guidance Counselors:
Mr. Eric Novelle-Smith – C.V. Bethel Senior High School
Ms. Dellerease Bethel – H.O. Nash Junior High School

Artists: Antonia Deveaux – C.V. Bethel Senior High School
Timothy Kabiga – St. Anne's High School
Charlton Strachan – Doris Johnson Senior High School

Tatyana Pratt – Aquinas College
Sasha Stuart – Aquinas College
Kimberley Stuart – Aquinas College
Gabriele Nicholas Josephs – Mary Star Catholic Academy
Sabrina Josephs - Parent
Paloma Cartwright – NGM Major High School
Sharana Gray – Inagua All Age School Celestia Austin
Shaqnell Rasha' Knowles – C.V. Bethel Senior High School
Lenice Johnson – C.V. Bethel Senior High School
Aaliyah Miller – C.V. Bethel Senior High School
Nigia Mackey – C.V. Bethel Senior High School
Makail Carey – C.V. Bethel Senior High School
Mrs. Cylestina Williams – Subject Coordinator, Debate Coach, C.I. Gibson Senior High School
Mrs. Abigail Ralph – Debate Coach, C.I. Gibson Senior High School
Ms. Shanika Rolle – Debate Coach, C.I. Gibson Senior High School
Fetenel Francois – C.I. Gibson Senior High School
Stanesha Deligence – C.I. Gibson Senior High School
Donnisha M. Johnson – C.I. Gibson Senior High School
Jesskika Christophe – C.I Gibson Senior High School
Lincey Catwright – C.I. Gibson Senior High School
Leander Albury – C.I. Gibson Senior High School
Ashley Gowie – C.I. Gibson Senior High School
Jonniece Saunders – C.I. Gibson Senior High School
Troy Trembley – Doris Johnson Senior High School
Maggie Milford – Parent

INTRODUCTION

Students entering Senior High School often do so with reservation and trepidation; this is a crucial step for any child. Children may feel fearful and anxious about going to a new school and a new environment. There will be new students and new teachers they will get to know. Students will take more subjects than they were taking in Junior High School.

The objective of this book is to help the grade 10 student settle as quickly as possible, so he/she can be about the business of learning. Every school age child in Senior High School, in the Commonwealth of The Bahamas, from Inagua in the south to Grand Bahama in the north, can benefit from using this book.

The activities are designed in a way that in the absence of a Guidance Counselor, the student, with the help of the Homeroom teacher, Family Life teacher, and parent can still use the materials in this book. The information required will place the counselor or teacher in a better position to assist the student.

From this book, the student will:
a. Learn ways to help him/her successfully survive Senior High School.
b. Learn how to improve study skills to perform better in school.
c. Learn about graduation requirements to obtain The Bahamas High School Diploma.
d. Learn useful Drug Awareness information.
e. Learn how to use the internet properly.
f. Find helpful information about sexuality.
g. Learn money management skills.

The grade 10 student will learn valuable skills that will be beneficial to him/her for the rest of his/her life.

Additionally, parents are asked to play an active role in the life of their child by utilizing the tools included in this book. These helpful tools will help each parent monitor the progress of his/her child.

I wish a smooth transition into Senior High School for each child and parent who uses this book.

C.D. Minnis

7 Reasons the Student Needs This Book:

1. You will **SETTLE** quickly into the rudiments of your new school.

2. You will **CULTIVATE** school spirit for your new school.

3. You will set **EXPECTATIONS** and **GOALS** for yourself, and you will **DETERMINE** how you will achieve them.

4. You will form a closer **BOND** with your parents.

5. You will **UNDERSTAND** and **APPRECIATE** the role of your Guidance Counselor /teacher.

6. You will **GET ALONG** with friends and classmates.

7. You will be a **SUPERSUCCESSFUL** student.

7 Reasons Parents Need This Book:

1. You will be able to monitor the **SUCCESS** of your child's academic performance.

2. You will **PARTNER** with the school to ensure the success of your child.

3. You will be more **AWARE** of challenges your child may be experiencing in school.

4. You will be more **INVOLVED** in the development of your child's physical, mental, spiritual and social life.

5. You will **UNDERSTAND** your child needs you, as a parent, to be actively involved in his/her life.

6. You will form a **CLOSER BOND** with your child.

7. You will **APPRECIATE** the important role the Guidance Counselor/teacher plays in the life of your child.

7 Reasons the Guidance Counselor/ Teacher Needs This Book:

1. You will be more **SUCCESSFUL** with your students.

2. You will have more **CONTACT** with your students' parents.

3. You will work **CLOSER** with administrators and teachers.

4. You will feel **BETTER** about your role in the life of the students.

5. You will be better **ORGANIZED**.

6. You will feel **LESS STRESSED**.

7. You will be more **RESPECTED** as a professional.

Table of Contents

Chapter 1...Welcome to Senior High School	11
Chapter 2...Grade 10-Results Oriented	16
Chapter 3...Your Guidance Counselor	22
Chapter 4...Graduation Requirements	26
Chapter 5...Study Skills	32
Chapter 6...Your Future is in Your Hands	39
Chapter 7...Healthy Living	44
Chapter 8...Drug Awareness	49
Chapter 9...Proper Use of the Internet, Social Media & Cell Phones	55
Chapter 10...Money Management	61
Chapter 11...Parental Involvement	66
Appendix A...Student Progress Report	72
Appendix B...Emergency Contact Numbers	73
Appendix C...School Supplies	74
Appendix D...Student Information Sheet	75
Appendix E...Group Counseling Consent Form	77
Appendix F...Individual Counseling Consent Form	79
Appendix G...Certificate of Completion	81

SENIOR HIGH SCHOOL

Chapter 1
Welcome to Senior High School

Letter to Parent/Guardian

Dear Parent/Guardian,

We are starting chapter 1 on _____ (Date).

In this chapter, your child will learn new and exciting information about his/her new school. The school's Senior Master or Mistress will speak on the importance of obeying the school's rules. Additionally, a police officer will be invited to present to the students on rules and laws.

By the end of this chapter, your child will learn why it is important to keep order in the classroom, the school, the community and in the country.

Warmest regards,

_____
Guidance Counselor/Teacher

BONDING ACTIVITY

Name three former principals of your school and the years they served. Take your child to the public library to research this information.

1. _____
   _____
2. _____
   _____
3. _____
   _____

Jeremiah 29:11-"For I know the plans I have for you, declares the Lord, plans to prosper you, and not for evil, to give you a future and hope."

Description of my new school

The name of my Senior High School is _____

Which year did your school open? _____

Who is your school named after? _____

What was his/her profession? _____

List at least three persons who served as principal of your school:

1. _____
2. _____
3. _____

My first year at _____ will be _____

(Name of school)

(Happy, productive, meaningful, positive, etc. or use your own descriptive to fill in the blank)

THE ADMINISTRATIVE TEAM- A Principal heads the school. Your school may have two Vice-Principals, two Senior Masters, and two Senior Mistresses.
1. My new Principal's name is _____
2. The Vice-Principals' names are _____
   and _____
3. The Senior Masters' names are _____
   and _____
4. The Senior Mistresses' names are _____
   and _____

HOMEROOM TEACHER - You may have one or two homeroom teachers who will mark you present each day when you are at school and absent when you are not at school. Your homeroom teacher(s) may be one of your subject teachers, as well.
1. My homeroom teachers' names are _____
   and _____
2. My homeroom is _____ (E.g., 10C), and we are in room _____
3. There are _____ students in my homeroom class.
4. Which house are you in? _____
5. My house color is _____

My School's Vision Statement: _____
_____

My School's Mission Statement: _____
_____

The School's Prayer: _____
_____

The School's Pledge: _____
_____

The School's Motto: _____

The Words of the School's Song:
_____
_____
_____
_____
_____
_____
_____
_____

Paste a picture of the School's Mascot in the space:

Instruction: Students will create a commercial/advertisement, brochure or flyer outlining the school's rules.

SCHOOL NURSE - The nurse is assigned to your school in case of a medical emergency during the day. The nurse can refer you for further help from a doctor or hospital.

The name of my school's nurse is
_____

SECURITY OFFICER(S) – The security officer(s) are stationed at the entrance of your school to check all visitors coming on campus to ensure they do not harm you. Periodically, the security officer(s) will patrol the campus to make sure you are safe.

The names of my school's security officers are
1. _____
2. _____

The support staff will help maintain a clean, green and pristine environment for you to learn and grow in. Name your school's support staff. Our janitors are
1. _____
2. _____
3. _____
4. _____
5. _____

The yardman is
_____

I acknowledge my child has successfully completed chapter 1.

_____   _____
Parent/Guardian's Signature   Date

Chapter 2
Grade 10 – Results Oriented

Letter to Parent/Guardian

Dear Parent/Guardian,

    We are starting chapter 2 on _____ (Date).

    In this section, we will look at your child's daily timetable. You will also learn about various examinations, both national and international, that your child will take while attending this high school.

Warmest regards,

_____
Guidance Counselor/Teacher

BONDING ACTIVITY

Encourage your child to sign up with the school's Guidance Counselor for the PSAT/NMSQT and/or the ACT plan. Assist your child with logging on to www.collegeboard.org and www.actstudent.org.

Date for the PSAT/NMSQT:

_____

Date for the ACT Plan:

_____

Romans 8:28 – "And we know that all things work together for good to those who love God, to those who are the called according to His purpose."

Heraclitus, the Pre-Socratic Greek philosopher, says, "The only thing constant is change." You have started Senior High School, and your Junior High school days are behind you. How do you cope with these changes? Do you join a club or organization? Do you take new and challenging classes? Do you socialize with new friends?

List two things you will do to adjust to Senior High School.
1. _____
2. _____

List four interesting things about your Junior School:	List four interesting things about your Senior School:	Similarities between your Junior School and Senior School:
1._____ 2._____ 3._____ 4._____	1._____ 2._____ 3._____ 4._____	1._____ 2._____ 3._____ 4._____

EXERCISE AND TEXTBOOKS - You will need to have a different exercise book for each subject. You will study more subjects in Senior High School than you did in Junior High School. You will have a different teacher for each subject. You will remain in these classes for your Senior High School years. You will be exposed to subjects such as Physics, Chemistry, Combined Science, Agriculture, Dance, Handbells, Calculus, Geography, History, Religious Studies and many others for the first time.

	STUDENT'S TIMETABLE				
	MONDAY	TUESDAY	WEDNESDAY	THURSDAY	FRIDAY
PERIOD 1 SUBJECT TEACHER ROOM	_____ _____ _____	_____ _____ _____	_____ _____ _____	_____ _____ _____	_____ _____ _____
PERIOD 2 SUBJECT TEACHER ROOM	_____ _____ _____	_____ _____ _____	_____ _____ _____	_____ _____ _____	_____ _____ _____
PERIOD 3 SUBJECT TEACHER ROOM	_____ _____ _____	_____ _____ _____	_____ _____ _____	_____ _____ _____	_____ _____ _____
PERIOD 4 SUBJECT TEACHER ROOM	_____ _____ _____	_____ _____ _____	_____ _____ _____	_____ _____ _____	_____ _____ _____
PERIOD 5 SUBJECT TEACHER ROOM	_____ _____ _____	_____ _____ _____	_____ _____ _____	_____ _____ _____	_____ _____ _____

BREAK: _____ a.m. - _____ a.m.
LUNCH: _____ p.m. - _____ p.m.

TESTS AND QUIZZES - Your teachers will test periodically to ensure you understand the lessons. The Bahamas General Certificate of Secondary Education (**B.G.C.S.E.**) examinations will be administered in either grades 10, 11 or 12 depending on the school's policy for allowing students to sit external examinations. Also, students who were not successful at passing their Bahamas Junior Certificate (B.J.C.) examinations in Junior High School may be allowed to take them in Senior High School.

Art & Craft	Art & Design & Craft	Art & Design	Auto Mechanics
Biology	Bookkeeping/Accounts	Carpentry & Joinery	Chemistry
Clothing Construction	Combined Science	Commerce	Economics
Electrical Installation	English Language	Food & Nutrition	French
Geography	Graphical Communication	History	Literature
Mathematics	Music	Office Procedures	Physics
Religious Studies	Spanish	Typewriting	

Ministry of Education - The Commonwealth of The Bahamas
in collaboration with
University of Cambridge Local Examinations Syndicate

Bahamas General Certificate of Secondary Education

This is to certify that the candidate named below sat the Bahamas General Certificate of Secondary Education Examination and reached at least Grade G in the subject(s) named.

1930/

C. V. BETHEL HIGH

LITERATURE	B (b)
ENGLISH LANGUAGE	B (b)
BIOLOGY	A (a)
CHEMISTRY	A (a)
COMBINED SCIENCE	A (a)
PHYSICS	A (a)
SPANISH	A (a)

SUBJECTS RECORDED: SEVEN

Examination of May 20

Director of Education
Ministry of Education

Vice-Chancellor
University of Cambridge

Examination and Assessment Division, Ministry of Education Bahamas

Candidate's Signature

School No: 1930   Candidate No: Date of Birth: N.I.B: 00000000

Certificate No: 000000

Additionally, you may write the following College Board examinations:
1. Grades 10 or 11 – Preliminary Scholastic Aptitude Test (PSAT/NMSQT)
2. Grades 11 or 12 – Scholastic Aptitude Test (SAT)
3. Grade 12 – Advanced Placement (AP)

You may also take the following American College Test:
1. Grade 10 – ACT Plan
2. Grade 11 & 12 - ACT

Some Senior High Schools administer the Pitman examinations, RSA examinations and the International Baccalaureate (IB) examinations.

Instruction: To promote school spirit, students will create a 4-minute Photo Story about their new school entitled, *"My school is the best school in The Bahamas."*

Photo courtesy of www.abacobahamas.com

Columbus Landing, San Salvador, Bahamas
"Don't be afraid to discover uncharted waters." C.D. Minnis

I acknowledge my child has successfully completed chapter 2.

_____   _____

Parent/Guardian's Signature   Date

Chapter 3
Your Guidance Counselor

Letter to Parent/Guardian

Dear Parent/Guardian,

    We are starting chapter 3 on _____ (Date).

    In this chapter, we will learn the important role the Guidance Counselor plays in the school. Your child will understand and appreciate he/she can always seek the assistance of the counselor for personal/social issues, academic help and career planning.

Warmest regards,

_____
Guidance Counselor/Teacher

BONDING ACTIVITY
List at least four ways your child may receive assistance from the Guidance Counselor.

1. _____

2. _____

3. _____

4. _____

Proverbs 1:5 – "Let the wise hear and increase in learning and the one who understands obtain guidance."

Your school may have more than one Guidance Counselor. Your Guidance Counselor will work along with the Administrative team and your teachers to ensure you have a meaningful Senior High School experience.

WHEN DO YOU NEED TO SEE YOUR GUIDANCE COUNSELOR?
- Are you anxious about your new school and finding it difficult to adjust?
- Do you feel overwhelmed by being in a bigger school with more students?
- Do you feel as though there are too many subjects for you to learn?

These are all good reasons to visit your Guidance Counselor.

Talk To Your Counselor. Sometimes it is hard to trust other people. Your school counselor will help you overcome shyness, resist peer pressure and deal with stress. You are not alone. You can trust your counselor who will be there for you.

What's On Your Mind?
Are you having trouble in school?
Are you getting along with other students?
Are you being bullied?
Are you worried about something that is happening at home?
Think about what you want to talk about so that you can tell your counselor everything and get help.

Listen To Your Counselor. Depending on the reason you are visiting your counselor, you may get possible solutions to a problem. You and your counselor will brainstorm together and figure out several ideas for solving your problem. Your counselor might have to call your parents to help work out the problem. The solution will only work if you listen to your counselor, and then make a commitment to follow through with necessary changes.

Be Open and Honest. Benjamin Franklin said, "Honesty is the Best Policy." Always tell the truth even when it may get you in trouble. It is easier for your counselor to get to the bottom of a problem if you are honest. However, being open is a little different from being honest. When you are open, it means you are saying what is on your mind. So, you must be open and honest if you want your counselor to help you.

COUNSELORS CAN ASSIST YOU IN MAKING SOUND DECISIONS: Talk to your counselor if you have academic challenges, problems with others, alcohol or other drug abuse, sexuality challenges or depression. Your counselor will also assist you with deciding upon your future career.

You are always welcomed in the counselor's office, so make an appointment or just drop in to see your counselor today.

I acknowledge my child has successfully completed chapter 3.

_____   _____
Parent/Guardian's Signature   Date

Minnis / Secondary School / 26

CHAPTER 4
GRADUATION REQUIREMENTS

Letter to Parent/Guardian

Dear Parent/Guardian,

    We are starting chapter 4 on _____ (Date).

    In this section, your child will learn about the requirements to obtain The Bahamas High School Diploma if he/she attends a public school. If your child attends a private school, speak with the Guidance Counselor to find out the requirements for graduating from that school. It is imperative your child understands from day one the requirements for graduation.

    Also, your child will learn about continuing his/her education after high school or joining the ranks of the employed. Persons from various local colleges/universities will be invited to speak about their institution. Additionally, representatives from the Scholarships Unit, Lyford Cay Foundation, Chance Foundation and Public Schools Scholars Programme, etc., will also be invited to enlighten students about scholarships their organizations offer.

Warmest regards,

_____
Guidance Counselor/Teacher

BONDING ACTIVITY

Assist your child with creating a checklist of graduation requirements at his/her school.

1. _____
2. _____
3. _____
4. _____
5. _____
6. _____
7. _____
8. _____

Deuteronomy 31:6 - "So be strong and courageous! Do not be afraid, and do not panic before them. For the Lord, your God will personally go ahead of you. He will neither fail you nor abandon you."

Graduation requirements are standard in all Government schools. However, the requirements vary in private schools. Below is the list of CRITERIA to EARN a BAHAMAS HIGH SCHOOL DIPLOMA:

CUMULATIVE GPA – Students must obtain a cumulative GPA of 2.00 or higher on a 4.00 scale. This is calculated over THREE (3) years: Grades ten (10), eleven (11) and twelve (12).

90 % ATTENDANCE & PUNCTUALITY – Students need 90% attendance and punctuality recorded over a three-year period (Grades 10 – 12).

27 CREDIT HOURS – Students must attain 27 credit hours over a three-year period (Grades 10-12).

PARENT/GUARDIAN INVOLVEMENT – Parent/Guardian must attend at least one of the scheduled parent/teacher meetings planned by the school during each of the 3 years (Grades 10 – 12).

B.J.C. EXAMINATIONS – Students must attain at least four (4) B.J.C.'s inclusive of Mathematics, English Language, a Science and Social Science or a career or technical subject with a D pass or higher.

JOB READINESS TRAINING - Students must complete 20 hours of Job Readiness Training in grades 10 and 11.

COMMUNITY SERVICE – 30 hours of Community Service must be completed in grade 10.

Begin high school with the end in mind. What will you do when you graduate? Will you go on to postsecondary education? Will you go to the University of The Bahamas, Bahamas Technical & Vocational Institute, Bahamas Agriculture & Marine Science Institute (BAMSI), National Training Agency (NTA), LJM Maritime Academy, or College or University abroad? Will you look for a job? Where will you work? Will it be in Nassau, or a Family Island, or maybe in the United States? What about working in a private firm or for the government?

        Decisions!   Decisions!   Decisions!

But, whatever you decide to do, you must complete high school.

THE UNIVERSITY OF THE BAHAMAS (UB): The University of The Bahamas offers a broad range of programs. You can receive an Associate Degree, a Bachelor's Degree or a Master's Degree in various professions. Additionally, the University offers enrichment programs.

BAHAMAS TECHNICAL & VOCATIONAL INSTITUTE: Perhaps you want to study a trade. The Bahamas Technical and Vocational Institute (BTVI) is the place for you.

BAHAMAS AGRICULTURE & MARINE SCIENCE INSTITUTE (BAMSI): This institute provides professional and technical qualifications for various branches of agriculture and marine resources.

NATIONAL TRAINING AGENCY (NTA): The National Training Agency offers skills training in a number of areas: Butler Services, Domestic Technician, Non-Instructional Teacher's Aide, Food and Beverage, Housekeeping, Customer Service, Allied Health Care, etc.

FULL-TIME EMPLOYMENT: You don't want to go on to college/university or a trade school, but you want to work. Be prepared, do your research about the company first to ensure it will be the right fit for you.

Education is expensive. Do you know how you are going to fund your tertiary education? Can your parents afford to pay for a college/university education? Will you need scholarships to pay for your college/university education? You need to begin researching scholarship opportunities now.

1. Bursary Scholarship – Students with 5 or more B.G.C.S.E.'s with C grade or higher including Mathematics and English are eligible to receive this scholarship to attend the University of the Bahamas.
2. Lyford Cay Foundation – offers a myriad of technical & academic scholarships.
3. Chance Foundation – provides technical & academic scholarships.
4. Public Schools Scholars Programme – Students with 5 or more B.G.C.S.E.'s, SAT and ACT required scores can vie for an opportunity to receive this scholarship.

If you're an athlete, please research athletic associations like the NCAA, NAIA and the NJCAA for their rules, regulations and eligibility guidelines.

Recipients of the 2016 Public School Scholars Scholarship Programme

TRANSCRIPT: Your transcript will be one of the most important documents you will need upon completing high school. It is necessary when applying to college/university, for scholarships, or a job. Your transcript will have your Senior High School grades. However, the institution you are applying to may also need your grades from Junior High School. It is important you maintain good grades throughout high school. Your cumulative grade point average (GPA) is vital. Your cumulative GPA will be an average of your six (6) terms in Senior High School.

PHONE: (242)321-0758   (242)398-3930 (FAX)   P.O. BOX SS-5056

BAHAMAS SENIOR HIGH SCHOOL
THOMPSON STREET, NASSAU, BAHAMAS
MINISTRY OF EDUCATION
OFFICIAL SENIOR SCHOOL TRANSCRIPT

SCHOOL'S PROFILE: Bahamas Senior High School is a three-year public school with an enrollment of 700 students from grades 10-12. The school opened in 1984 and is accredited by the Ministry of Education. Students can graduate with a Bahamas High School Diploma, as well as B.J.C., B.G.C.S.E., SAT, ACT and AP Exams.

NAME OF STUDENT:	FIRST: Jane	MIDDLE: Lavette		SURNAME: Doe	
ADDRESS:	STREET: 35 Honeyburn Lane	P.O. BOX: FH-2910		ISLAND: New Providence	
DATE OF BIRTH:	MONTH: October	DAY: 17	YEAR: 2000	SEX: Female	
PARENT/GUARDIAN:	Harold and Jenny Doe			DATE OF ENTRY: September 2014	
TELEPHONE: 394-0000/471-0000	EMAIL ADDRESS: janedoe@hotmail.com			DATE OF LEAVING: June 2017	

ACADEMIC RECORD

SUBJECTS	10-1 SG	10-2 SG	10 CR	11-1 SG	11-2 SG	11 CR	12-1 SG	12-2 SG	12 CR	KEY: SG: SCHOLASTIC GRADE CR: CREDIT		
ENGLISH LANGUAGE	B	B	1	B	B	1	B	B	1			
MATHEMATICS	B	B	1	B	B	1	B	A	1	**GRADING SCALE**		
BIOLOGY	A	B	1	A	A	1	B	B	1	Grade	Percentage	Points
CIVICS	A	A	.5	A	A	.5	A	A	.5	A	100%-90%	4.0
PHYSICAL EDUCATION	A	A	1	A	A	.5	A	B	.5	B	89%-71%	3.0
ACCOUNTS	A	A	1	B	B	1	A	A	1	C	70%-56%	2.0
COMPUTER SCIENCE	A	A	1	A	A	1	A	A	1	D	55%-45%	1.0
COMMERCE	B	B	1	C	B	1	B	B	1	F	44%-0%	0.0
CRAFT	A	A	1	A	A	1	A	A	1	Cumulative GPA – 3.57		
HISTORY	A	A	1	A	B	1	A	B	1	Credits – 27.5		
GPA & CREDITS	3.70	3.60	9	3.50	3.50	9	3.60	3.50	9			

EXAMINATIONS KEY: B.J.C.-Bahamas Junior Certificate   B.G.C.S.E. Bahamas General Certificate of Education
ACT-American College Test   SAT-Scholastic Aptitude Test   AP-Advanced Placement

YEAR	B.J.C. SUBJECTS	GRADE	YEAR	B.G.C.S.E. SUBJECTS	GRADE
June 2014	ENGLISH LANGUAGE	A	June 2016	ENGLISH LANGUAGE	B
June 2014	MATHEMATICS	A	June 2016	BOOKKEEPING & ACCOUNTS	A
June 2014	SOCIAL STUDIES	A	June 2016	MATHEMATICS	A
June 2014	GENERAL SCIENCE	A	June 2016	KEYBOARDING	A
June 2014	HEALTH SCIENCE	A	June 2016	HISTORY	B
June 2014	ENGLISH LITERATURE	B	June 2016	CRAFT	A
June 2014	CRAFT	A			

EXAMINATIONS	DATE	READING	MATHEMATICS	WRITING SKILLS	SCIENCE
SAT SCORES					
ACT SCORES					
AP SUBJECTS/SCORES	SUBJECT:		SCORE:	SUBJECT:	SCORE:
AP SUBJECTS/SCORES	SUBJECT:		SCORE:	SUBJECT:	SCORE:

HONORS, PRIZES, AWARDS: Principal's Award, Computer Award, Head Girl	EXTRA CURRICULAR ACTIVITIES: Business Club, GGYA, Debate Team	OFFICES HELD: Head Girl, President of Debate Team & Business Club
COMMUNITY SERVICE (30 HOURS): Pat's Senior Citizens Home	JOB READINESS (20 HOURS): ☐ Complete ☐ Incomplete	EDUCATIONAL/VOCATIONAL PLANS: To become a Certified Public Accountant
COMMENTS: Jane Doe entered Bahamas Senior High School in September 2014 and graduated June 2017. Her cumulative G.P.A. is 3.57. She has met the 90% attendance and punctuality requirement for graduation.		MEDICAL CONDITION: No known medical condition.

PRINCIPAL/VICE PRINCIPAL: GUIDANCE COUNSELOR:

DATE:

> THINKING ABOUT DROPPING OUT OF SCHOOL?
> THINK AGAIN!
> Graduating from high school means more than getting a diploma. Staying in school will help you:
> - Learn about yourself.
> - Develop your talents.
> - Learn about essential job skills.
> - Decide what you want to do in the future.

Each student will research the school he/she wants to attend after graduating from High School, and list the requirements to attend the school of their choice. Students will also do research on the different scholarships available with concentration on scholarships available in their preferred intended major in college. (E.g., culinary students may wish to apply for the CHTAEF)

St. Stephen's Anglican Church, November 2009 – Fresh Creek, Andros, Bahamas
"Keep yourself grounded in Christ." C.D. Minnis
(This church was destroyed by fire May 2010)

I acknowledge my child has successfully completed chapter 5.

_____   _____
Parent/Guardian's Signature   Date

Chapter 5
Study Skills

Letter to Parent/Guardian

Dear Parent/Guardian,

    We are starting chapter 5 on _____ (Date).

    In this chapter, your child will learn how to develop sound study habits. He/she will also learn tips on how to study for examinations.

Warmest regards,

_____
Guidance Counselor/Teacher

BONDING ACTIVITY

Sit with your child and create a workable study timetable your child will be able to follow every day.

Day	Time	Time	Time	Time
Monday				
Tuesday				
Wednesday				
Thursday				
Friday				
Saturday				
Sunday				

John 13:17 – "If you know these things, blessed are you if you do them."

"Students learn 10% of what they read, 20% of what they hear, 30% of what they see, 50% of what they see and hear, 70% of what is discussed with others, 80% of what they experience personally, and 95% of what they teach to someone else." William Glasser

Complete the questionnaire below to see how you may be affected by various conditions.

	Check the most appropriate answers.	Yes	No
1.	Unreliable bus service.		
2.	Spend too much time on social media, e.g., Facebook, WhatsApp, etc.		
3.	Watch too much television.		
4.	Lack of money to buy textbooks.		
5.	Teachers are regularly absent.		
6.	No interest in the subject(s) taught.		
7.	Classes too noisy – too many distractions.		
8.	Classes too big – challenging for the teacher to give individualized attention.		
9.	Too many responsibilities at home.		
10.	No lunch or money to purchase lunch.		
11.	Too many extra-curricular activities (clubs, sports teams, etc.).		
12.	Part-time job consumes too much time.		

KNOW YOUR LEARNING STYLE

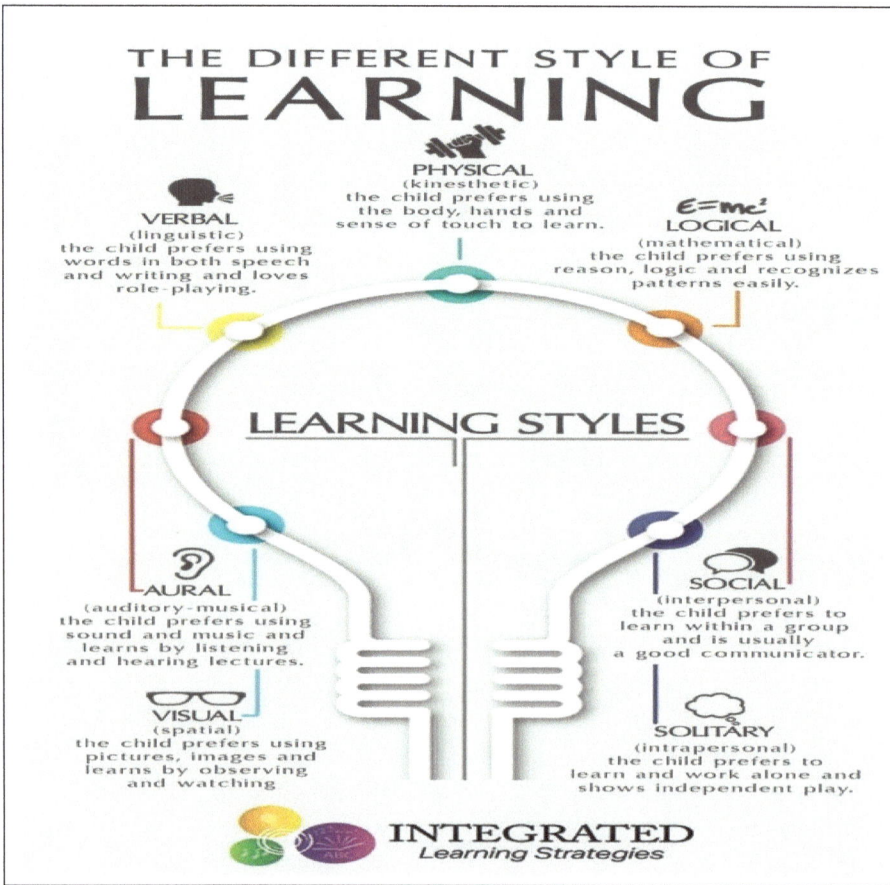

"Every child has a different Learning style and pace. Each child is unique, not only capable of learning, but also capable of succeeding."

Robert John Meehan

TIPS TO HELP YOU ACHIEVE EXCELLENT GRADES

The following will help you improve your grades or maintain the good grades you are achieving:
1. Group work – create focus groups, e.g., Math, Science groups, etc.
2. Create study groups on Facebook, WhatsApp or any favorite social media.
3. Seek help – peer tutoring or professional tutoring.
4. Use past examination papers – B.G.C.S.E., B.J.C.

A well-rounded student is one who is not just book smart. Well-rounded students are involved in clubs and organizations. To maximize their exposure and network with other students, they take part in various competitions, such as:
1. Junior Minister of Tourism Competition
2. Financial Sector Competitions
3. Essay Competitions
4. Debate Competitions

C.I. Gibson Senior High School Debate Team
2016 National Debate Champions

The Following Will Cause Poor Concentration:

Noise	Dislike of subject	Constant interruptions
Study area	Phone/iPad	Poor attention span
Boredom	T.V.	Unwillingness to study
Daydreaming	Computer	Lack of sleep
Hunger	Music	Poor diet
Worry	Lack of interest	

Study! Study! Study some more. You will have to study every night. However, you should do assigned homework first. You must read over all the work you did during the day, and read ahead for the upcoming lessons. Then follow your study timetable. As you prepare to create your study schedule keep in mind all the activities you have each day.

E.g., Tuesdays – 3:00 p.m. – 5:00 p.m.: Band practice
      Thursdays – 3:15 p.m. – 4:15 p.m.: Track practice
      Saturdays – 9:00 a.m. – 11:00 a.m.: Basketball practice

STUDY TIMETABLE

TIME	4p.m.-5p.m.	5p.m.-6p.m.	6p.m.-7p.m.	7p.m.-8p.m.	8p.m.-9p.m.	9p.m.-10p.m.
MONDAY		MATHS		PE		
TUESDAY					SS	
WEDNESDAY		ENGLISH		SCIENCE		
THURSDAY				CIVICS		
FRIDAY						

TIME	9a.m.-10a.m.	10a.m.-11a.m.	11a.m.-12p.m.	12p.m.-1p.m.	1p.m.-2p.m.	2p.m.-3p.m.	3p.m.-4p.m.
SATURDAY						ACCOUNTS	
SUNDAY							

TIME	4p.m.-5pm	5p.m.-6p.m.	6p.m.-7p.m.	7p.m.-8p.m.	8p.m.-9p.m.	9p.m.-10p.m.
SATURDAY						
SUNDAY	CRAFT					

HOW TO ACE YOUR TESTS

1. SKIM THE TEST QUICKLY. Knowing what is on the test will help you budget your time wisely.
2. READ THE DIRECTIONS CAREFULLY. If you are not clear about something in the instructions, ask.
3. DON'T BE AFRAID TO SKIP A QUESTION. Answer questions you are confident of first. Come back if you have time to respond to the questions you did not answer.
4. LOOK FOR "CLUE WORDS." On a multiple choice or true/false test, words such as always, none, all and everybody usually means you can eliminate that choice.
5. CHECK YOUR WORK. Make sure you have crossed your T's and dotted your I's. Careless mistakes like these lead to wrong answers.

Courtesy of "The Parent Institute."

Your teachers will test to see how well you understood the objectives of the lessons and to measure your understanding of the lesson taught.

What to do before test day:
Match the correct answer on the right with the stem on the left.

STEM	ANSWER
1._____ Make a "Study Sheet"	A. Review for the test with one or more friends.
2._____ Dress for success	B. Studying the night before the exam for the first time.
3._____ Make flash cards	C. Create your test by thinking of questions the teacher may ask on the examination.
4._____ Eat breakfast	D. Write key facts about each subject, e.g., Formulas in Math or Science dates in history.
5._____ Create a Practice Test	E. Eat the morning of the test.
6._____ Study with a buddy	F. Wear comfortable clothes on test day.
7._____ Take the supplies you need	G. Write points to review everything from vocabulary words to math facts.
8._____ Do not cram	H. Set out everything you will need the night before.

Courtesy of "The Parent Institute."

SUCCESSFUL STUDENTS REWARDED

Students who work hard are rewarded with excellent grades. Successful students are on the Honor Roll, The Principal's List, The Dean's List and are usually high achievers in and out of school.

- At the Olympics - achievement is measured by obtaining gold, silver or bronze medals.
- In Bahamian Tourism Industry - success is measured by winning a Cacique Award.
- Bahamian success - achievement is measured by winning a Bahamian Icon Award.
- Best performance in the theater - success is measured by winning an Academy Award.

Instruction: Each student will create a jingle, poem or picture story of what he/she will do to become a success story.

Place a check mark (√) in each box to indicate the tasks you have completed successfully.

Name: _____	M	T	W	T	F	My personal goal for this week is _____ checks out of 50.
I finished homework.						My total score this week was ___
I studied at least one hour at home.						Write an assessment of your week.
I finished classwork.						
I attended all classes today.						
I got to all classes on time today.						
I had all necessary materials.						
I displayed good behavior.						
I participated in class.						
I was respectful.						
I helped another student.						

Adapted from "Positive Classroom Management."

"To be a star, you must shine your light,
Follow your path and not be afraid of the darkness,
For that is when stars shine brightest." – Author unknown

Answer Key for "*How To Ace Your Tests*:" 1. D, 2. F, 3. G, 4. E, 5. C, 6. A, 7. H, 8. B

Salt Ponds, Inagua, Bahamas
"Your unique flavor makes the difference." C.D. Minnis

I acknowledge my child has successfully completed chapter 5.

_____   _____
Parent/Guardian's Signature   Date

Chapter 6
Your Future is in Your Hands

Letter to Parent/Guardian

Dear Parent/Guardian,

    We are starting chapter 6 on _____ (Date). In this chapter, your child will come to understand that for him/her to become successful in life, it is entirely up to him/her to make sound decisions that will positively affect his/her future.

    Your child will create a road map of how he/she will accomplish his/her goals, and begin working on achieving those goals now. Additionally, your child will understand that his/her gifts and talents should determine his/her future career.

Warmest regards,

_____
Guidance Counselor/Teacher

BONDING ACTIVITY

Assist your child with creating a Portfolio. Your child will continually add important accomplishments to the Portfolio.

- PHOTO
- BRIEF BIOGRAPHY
- COMPLETED JOB READINESS FORM (Grades 10 & 11)
- COMPLETED COMMUNITY SERVICE FORM (Grade 10)
- COMPLETED RESUME WITH AT LEAST THREE (3) REFERENCES
- COVER LETTER ATTACHED TO RESUME
- COMPLETED FORMS I.E. (APPLICATION FORMS, COLLEGE, JOBS)
- GOALS AND ACTION (HOW WILL THE GOALS BE ACHIEVED)
- FOUR SAMPLES OF CLASSWORK (ANY 4 SUBJECTS)
- A NEWSPAPER ARTICLE WITH A WRITTEN CRITIQUE
- CERTIFICATES EARNED (ATTENDANCE, SUBJECT, SPORTS, ETC.)
- POLICE CERTIFICATE
- HEALTH CERTIFICATE
- COPY OF PASSPORT
- COPY OF BIRTH CERTIFICATE, ETC.

Mark 10:27 – "With God all Things are Possible."
Psalm 51:10 - "Create in me a clean heart, O God; and renew a right spirit within me."

YOU CAN .... CHANGE THE WORLD!

> **Instructions: Draw a picture of you doing your favorite activity (e.g., playing a basketball game, video games, baking, etc.)   OR**
> **Create a collage of yourself using pictures from baby to present.**

"It's not what you call me that matters,
It's what I answer to that counts."
Allison Manswell

As a senior high school student, you must have a plan. Writing it down will help you visualize and accomplish your dreams.

IT'S ALL ABOUT ME
MY ROAD MAP TO SUCCESS...

THREE YEARS FROM NOW: YEAR _____

B.G.C.S.E. EXAMINATIONS SUBJECTS: PROJECTED GRADES:

_____   _____
_____   _____
_____   _____
_____   _____
_____   _____
_____   _____

COLLEGE_____   OR JOB_____

4 YEARS FROM NOW: YEAR _____
_____

8 YEARS FROM NOW: YEAR _____
_____

12 YEARS FROM NOW: YEAR _____

> **Instructions: Using the lyrics of one of the songs below, write what the words mean to you.**
> 1. *"I Can"* by Nas
> 2. *"Get Involved"* by Dr. Off
> 3. *"Scars To Your Beautiful"* by Alessia Cara
> 4. *"My Bahamian Thing"* by Ronnie Butler
> 5. *"Emancipate Yourself From Mental Slavery"* by Bob Marley
> 6. *"Keep The Vibe Alive"* by Geno D

Proverbs 18:16 – "A man's gifts make room for him and brings him before the great."

THE BEST CAREER FIT FOR YOU

> **A guest speaker from the Department of Labor will be invited to present to the class on the types of jobs needed in the country. Additionally, students will complete an interest and career survey to identify which area they are most passionate about. Students will come to appreciate how their talents and abilities will distinguish and set them apart from their peers and should be the deciding factor in choosing the career path they take.**

It is crucial for you to identify your passion early in high school. What do you enjoy doing most? What you love to do most should determine which career path you will take. Confucius says, "If you love what you do, you will never work a day in your life." Your future career should determine your pathway choice – the classes you must take to make a smooth transition to tertiary education or the job market easier.

How Can I Be Sure about my Career Choice?

Before you make any decisions, you should learn more about jobs in your interest areas. Some excellent ways to find out more are
* Surf the internet.
* Take a class related to your interest area.
* Volunteer in a career area that interests you.
* Job Experience/shadow.
* Talk to people who have jobs in your area of interest.
* Do research on jobs in your area of interest: salaries, tasks, expected openings, training requirement, opportunities for advancement, etc.

> **Instructions:** Students will research the needs of the country to determine if their career choice will assist in the development of The Bahamas. Also, each student will create a list of job requirements and salary for his/her dream career.

GOOD LUCK IN YOUR CAREER ADVENTURE

The Serenity Prayer
God grant me the Serenity to accept the things I cannot change,
Courage to change the things I can, And Wisdom to know the difference.
American theologian Reinhold Niebuhr (1892–1971).

LIVING THE BAHAMIAN DREAM

It is always important to dream. But, as you dream and plan your future always remember to be faithful to God, country, family and yourself.

Your school, the first computer, the first airplane, the first mall were all built because someone had a dream.

What do you dream about achieving in life? Create your "Bahamian Dream."

Instructions:
1. Make a list of all the things you want in life (good grades, career, iPhone, clothes, car, home, vacations, etc.)
2. Collect pictures of these items (look in magazines, computer)
3. Get a large poster board (Your favorite color)
4. Paste the photos on the board
5. Mount your dream board where you can see it every day to keep you motivated.

I acknowledge my child has successfully completed chapter 6.

_____   _____
Parent/Guardian's Signature   Date

Chapter 7
Healthy Living

Letter to Parent/Guardian

Dear Parent/Guardian,

    We are starting chapter 7 on _____ (Date).

    In this chapter, your child will learn about establishing a healthy relationship with both males and females. He/she will understand what it means to have a platonic relationship, and enjoy meaningful, productive and fun activities with his/her peers.

Warmest regards,

_____
Guidance Counselor/Teacher

BONDING ACTIVITY

Sit with your child and list some of the ways he/she can have clean and healthy fun with his/her peers.

1. _____
2. _____
3. _____
4. _____
5. _____
6. _____

1 Corinthians 6:19-20 – "Don't you realize that your body is the temple of the Holy Spirit, who lives in you and was given to you by God? You do not belong to yourself, for God bought you with a high price. So you must honor God with your body."

"Healthy Choices – A Healthier You"

One of the most rewarding relationships you can have is with someone of the opposite sex.

Being intimate with another person means not only giving up your body, but it involves the heart, mind, soul and emotions. You are still a teenager, and you are not ready for that level of intimacy.

Every year thousands of young girls and boys will make the decision to become sexually active. Unfortunately, in many cases, the consequences of becoming sexually active is often having a baby, sexually transmitted diseases and emotional stress.

Girls – get an education and become an independent adult. Young men – seek after getting the best education you can.

	Using assertive communication skills to say "no" or "use a condom."	Say No	Use a Condom	Comments
1.	An older 12th grade boy is dating a 10th grade girl; he wants her to have sex. What should she do?			
2.	A jitney driver asks a 10th grade student for her phone number so that he can date her. What should she do?			
3.	A 12th grade girl has been uncommonly kind to a 10th grade girl. Now she wants to date her. What should she do?			
4.	A 10th grade girl has been dating an older guy, and they are sexually active. They have never used a condom. She is now concerned about catching HIV or becoming pregnant. What should she do?			
5.	An older guy has befriended a male student. He gives him lots of money and buys him everything he wants. The older guy is pressuring him to have a relationship. What should he do?			
6.	A 12th grade female has been tutoring a 10th grade male student. It is evident she is attracted to him. What should he do?			
7.	A 10th grade boy is in a relationship with a 10th grade girl; they are sexually active. He has heard rumors that she is sleeping around. What should he do?			

Test yourself to see how ready you are for an intimate relationship:
If it does apply to you, check (√) Y. If it does not apply to you, check (√) N.

1. Y___ N___ You feel a need to belong.
2. Y___ N___ Teen sex goes against your religious belief.
3. Y___ N___ You believe in the saying, "no ringy, no tingy."
4. Y___ N___ You think it will make your boyfriend/girlfriend love you more.
5. Y___ N___ You cannot take care of yourself.
6. Y___ N___ It's just easier to say yes.
7. Y___ N___ You feel as if he/she will leave if you say no.
8. Y___ N___ Engaging in teenage sex goes against your parents' upbringing.
9. Y___ N___ You cannot take care of a child.
10. Y___ N___ All of your friends are having sex, so why not.
11. Y___ N___ You are trying to spite your parents.
12. Y___ N___ You are drunk or on drugs.
13. Y___ N___ You cannot wait to brag about having sex.
14. Y___ N___ It is just another "score."
15. Y___ N___ You do not like being a virgin.
16. Y___ N___ You do not know how to use protection – condoms, female contraceptives.
17. Y___ N___ You are not aware of the signs and symptoms of STI's and HIV.
18. Y___ N___ You think having "dry" sex is okay.
19. Y___ N___ You think pregnancy can't happen the first time.
20. Y___ N___ Teen sex goes against your moral beliefs.

Adapted from "The 7 Habits of Effective Teens" by Sean Covey

16 – 20 Yes: You are certainly not ready for any level of intimacy.
11 – 15 Yes: You are mature, but not mature enough to engage in this level of intimacy.
6 – 10 Yes: You have a fair understanding of what it means to be intimate, but not mature enough to engage in sexual intimacy.
0 – 5 Yes: You are not ready for any level of intimacy at your age.

TEN GREAT WAYS TO SHOW LOVE, WITHOUT HAVING SEX:

1. Talk on the phone for hours.
2. Group date – Go to the movies or parties in a group.
3. Study together.
4. Communicate on Facebook/Twitter, Whatsapp or email each other.
5. Be a member of the same club, Junior Achievement (JA), Youth Empowerment Program (YEP), Governor General Youth Award (GGYA), Science Club.
6. Exchange gifts.
7. Be silly – Laugh at each other's jokes.
8. Exchange pictures and post them in prominent places.
9. Tell your parents about the relationship.
10. Talk, talk and talk some more.

IT'S MY BODY, MY CHOICE -
NO TATTOOS FOR ME. LOVING ME

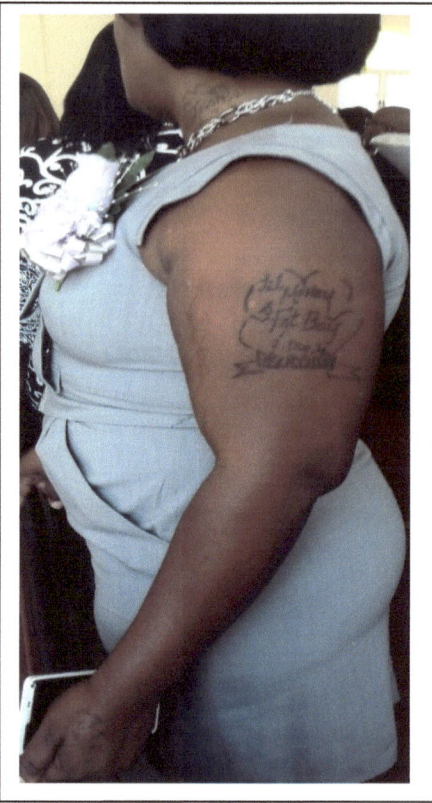

You must love and respect yourself before you can love and respect someone else. You must appreciate your worth and your value, and never sell yourself short.

It matters what you put in your body; it matters what you put on your body. Teens put tattoos on their bodies for the following reasons:

1. Their friends have tattoos.
2. A reward – e.g., for junior or senior school graduation.
3. _____
4. _____

Many people who placed tattoos on their bodies as teenagers, often grow up to regret that decision. Many hotels and business establishments will not employ individuals with visible tattoos on their body.

If you feel you must get a tattoo, make sure it is not placed on a visible area on your body that may hamper your progress in the future.

Instructions: Create a brochure outlining the effects of tattoos on the body.

Androsia Batik – Andros, Bahamas
"You are beautiful inside and outside." C.D. Minnis

I acknowledge my child has successfully completed chapter 7.

_____   _____
Parent/Guardian's Signature   Date

Chapter 8
Drug Awareness

Letter to Parent/Guardian

Dear Parent/Guardian,

    We are starting chapter 8 on _____ (Date).

    Drugs are extremely prevalent amongst teenagers. A guest speaker will be invited from the National Drug Council to present on the dangers of drugs. By the end of this chapter, your child will know the dangers of illicit drugs.

Warmest regards,

_____
Guidance Counselor/Teacher

BONDING ACTIVITY

Sit with your child and list some of the ways he/she can respond to friends or family who may offer him/her drugs to use or sell.

1. _____
2. _____
3. _____
4. _____
5. _____

Titus 2:6 – "Young people likewise exhort to be sober-minded."

65%
OF KIDS GET DRUGS FROM FRIENDS & FAMILY

1. Drugs are against the law. It is an illegal substance and if you are caught with it, you will face jail time. This criminal act could stop you from traveling to some countries, like the United States, in the future.
2. You do not function normally and cannot concentrate if you are under the influence of any drug.
3. Some drugs will lower sperm count in men and increase the risk of infertility in women.
4. Using drugs increases the risk of having an accident.
5. Drug use can result in a bad performance and poor grades in school.
6. Using drugs puts your future at risk.
7. Using drugs will distance you from your family and genuine friends.
8. Using drugs will not make you cool.
9. Taking drugs will not help you escape your problems; it will only create more.
10. If you know someone who has a drug problem, encourage your friend to get help.

Adapted from The Bahamas National Drug Council

Sir Sidney Poitier Bridge – Nassau, Bahamas

"You can conquer any problem." C.D. Minnis

Complete the Drug Awareness Crossword Puzzle to see how knowledgeable you are about drugs.

Drug Awareness Crossword Puzzle

Across

2. Sudden stoppage of drug use may result in this
6. Uncontrollable urge for drugs
7. Drinking alcohol may result in ulcers in this part of the body
9. Alcohol may cause osteoporosis
10. These drugs speed up your heart rate and breathing, e.g., Ritalin
12. Smoking may cause cirrhosis in this organ
13. Also known as Angel Dust

Down

1. Steps to take to help someone with a drug addiction
3. These drugs will cause irregular heartbeat, paranoid reactions, violent or suicidal thoughts and hallucinations, e.g., Prozac
4. Smoking may cause asthma, chronic bronchitis in this organ
5. The chemical in marijuana that causes the high
8. Examples of _____ are OxyContin, Fentanyl, Morphine, Demerol
11. These drugs slow down your brain and nervous system functions, example Xanax

15. Can be a confusing time for teenagers
18. A sign a teen may be on drugs
19. Drinking alcohol may result in a stroke
20. A result of taking drugs

14. Close family members may expose children to drugs
16. Smoking may inhibit formation of urine in this organ
17. A hallucinogen

Many teenagers will face the decision whether to take drugs in one form or the other. What will you do when confronted with this choice?

SCENARIO 1: Some school friends invited Philip, a tenth grade student, to a dance party. He is excited to go because this is the first time he has been invited to any event. His parents have given him permission to go. When he gets to the party, he feels uncomfortable and out of place. A girl he knows and likes offers him a "beedee" to smoke. She tells him it will relax him and help him to have fun.

> **Create a poster on the dangers of smoking.**

OR

SCENARIO 2: One of Serita's best friends, Pauline, has been drinking every weekend. She is now starting to drink during the week and has been late for school several mornings. She has been falling asleep during classes and is getting failing grades in many of her classes. Serita does not think Pauline's parents know what is happening.

> **Create a flyer on the dangers of drinking.**

Why do teenagers take drugs? Here are some of the reasons:

Fear
Anxiety
Low Self-Esteem
Escape from problems

Curiosity
Peer Pressure
Boredom

Signs to look for if your friends are using drugs:
1. Constant arguing, lying and rude behavior towards adults.
2. Wanting to be alone, keeping secrets, do not want to hang out anymore.
3. New unsavory friends.
4. Bad grades and poor school attendance.
5. Unkempt appearance.
6. Hyperactivity, drowsiness or forgetfulness.
7. Depression or mood swings.
8. Weight gain or weight loss.
9. Bloodshot eyes, use of eye-drops or a constant runny nose or coughing.
10. Money problems.

Adapted from "Teens drinking and drugs."

Drug Awareness Crossword Puzzle Answer Key

			1 T		2 W	I	T	H	D	R	A	W	3 A	L		
4 L			R										N			
U			E										T			
N			A		5 T		6 A	D	D	I	C	T	I	O	N	
G			T		H								D			
7 S	T	O	M	A	C	H		8 P		9 B	O	N	E	S		
			E					A					P			
			N					I					R			
	10 S	T	I	M	U	L	A	N	T	S			E		11 D	
							K						S		E	
						12 L	I	V	E	R			S		13 P	C P
					14 P		L						A		R	
					15 A	D	O	L	E	S	C	E	N	C	E	
16 K					R		E						T		S	
I				17 L	E		R						S		S	
18 D	R	O	W	S	I	N	E	S	S						A	
N				D		T						19 B	R	A	I	N
E						S									N	T
Y								20 T	R	E	M	O	R	S		

I acknowledge my child has successfully completed chapter 8.

_____   _____

Parent/Guardian's Signature   Date

Chapter 9
Proper Use of the Internet, Social Media & Cell Phones

Letter to Parent/Guardian

Dear Parent/Guardian,

    We are starting chapter 9 on _____ (Date).

    In this chapter, your child will learn about the benefits of properly using the internet. A guest speaker will be invited to address students on how the computer, social media and cell phones can make a positive difference or have a devastating impact on the life of your child.

Warmest regards,

_____
Guidance Counselor/Teacher

BONDING ACTIVITY

Sit with your child and list some of the ways he/she can use the internet to do schoolwork. Have your child list some ways he/she will never use the internet.

Positive ways to use the internet are
_____
_____
_____
_____
_____

Negative ways to use the internet are
_____
_____
_____
_____
_____

Ephesians 4:29 - *"Do not let any unwholesome talk come out of your mouths, but only what is helpful for building others up according to their needs, that it may benefit those who listen."*

The internet is an amazing tool that can help a student in many positive ways if used correctly.
- School work can be researched so that you can receive excellent grades.
- You can type and save your work on the computer and spell-check and grammar check to ensure errors in your assignments are kept to a minimum.
- You can copy and paste pictures off the internet into your schoolwork to enhance the overall appearance of it.
- You can download educational apps to help with homework and classwork.
- High school students can research colleges locally and abroad. You can sign onto the college or university's website and do a virtual tour of the college or university.
- Researching various examinations becomes a breeze. You can go online and do practice questions, which will assist you when writing multiple exams.

> **Directions:** Place students in groups of five (5). Each team will select one form of technology and show how their chosen technology can be used in the classroom.
> (Example of technology to choose from: iPhone, iPod, Game devices, Kindle, Smartphone, MP3 player, Computer, etc.)

Psalm 119:11 – "Thy word have I hid in mine heart, that I might not sin against thee."

When using the internet, you will be faced with many challenges such as:
- Internet addiction,
- pornography,
- violence,
- values not consistent with parents' upbringing,
- predators – including but not limited to pedophiles, criminals, etc.,
- cyberbullying and intimidation through social networks.

You are on the World Wide Web if you have:
- ever posted a comment or reply on the internet,
- uploaded a video to YouTube, WhatsApp, etc.,
- posted a picture on WhatsApp, Facebook, Twitter or any other social network.

Remember the world has access to the internet. Do not post naked pictures of yourself or others. Posting nude pictures can cause you to get in trouble with the law. It is called child pornography. More than 4.5 billion people use the internet and will have access to your information.

You submitted an application form for your "dream" job. You are all excited because you are qualified for the position. You did interns/ job shadowing in your field of study. You graduated with honors, and you are ready to start your dream job. Be aware your prospective employer will do a background check on you. One of the first places your perspective employer will look is on the internet. Also, the perspective college/university you plan to attend may google your name to do a background check on you.

When using the internet, ask yourself the following questions:
1. Would I embarrass or hurt anyone by what I posted?
2. How would my parents and teachers feel about what I posted?
3. Can legal actions be taken against me because of what I posted?
4. Can what I posted stop me from getting a job later in life?
5. How would I feel if what I posted was published in the media?
6. Do I have a clear conscience about what I posted?

CYBERBULLYING

One of the negative ways teenagers use the internet is to cyberbully. Warning signs of cyberbullying to watch for can include:
1. Emotional distress during or after using the Internet.
2. Withdrawal from friends and family members.
3. Avoidance of school or group gatherings.
4. Slipping grades and "acting out" in anger at home.
5. Changes in mood, behavior, sleep, or appetite.
6. Wanting to stop using the computer or cell phone.
7. Appearing nervous or jumpy when getting an instant message or email.

Courtesy of Saddleback Valley Unified School, *"Cyberbullying & Sexting – Parents Guide."*

Do not respond because doing so just fuels the fire and does not make the situation any better. You should keep the threatening messages, pictures, and texts, as these can be used as evidence with the bully's parents, school, employer, or even the police. If you are in the same class with the person who is cyberbullying you, tell your Guidance Counselor so something can be done right away to stop the bullying peacefully.

Adapted from "Cyberbullying: New problems, new tactics." www.kidshealth.org

If you are doing the cyberbullying, then you need to stop this negative behavior. This action might seem harmless but can hurt feelings and lead to grave consequences at home, school and in the community.

How do you react?

1. Your former friend has posted defamatory information about you on the internet. What do you do?
    a. Post defamatory information about this friend.
    b. Ignore it.
    c. Report the matter to your parents or Guidance Counselor.
    d. Confront the individual.

2. All your friends are posting sexually explicit pictures on the internet. They have been pressuring you to post some as well. You …
    a. Ignore their prompting.
    b. Post sexually explicit pictures of yourself.
    c. Drop them as friends.
    d. Tell your parents or Guidance Counselor.

3. Your boyfriend/girlfriend has been sex-texting you. What do you do?
   a. Drop him/her as a boyfriend/girlfriend.
   b. Sex-text him/her back.
   c. Tell him/her to stop it and mean it.
   d. Ignore the sex-text from him/her.

4. You recorded a fight between two of your former friends who you genuinely do not like. What do you do with the recording?
   a. Post the recording on WhatsApp.
   b. Send the recording to everyone in your contact list.
   c. Leave it on your phone for future use.
   d. Delete the recording from your phone.

5. Your friends are using their cell phones to trade answers during final exams. What do you do?
   a. Report the cheaters to the teacher.
   b. Tell your friends to stop cheating.
   c. Ignore what they are doing.
   d. Cheat along with them by trading answers on your cell phone too.

6. The substitute teacher has left the classroom unattended. Your friends are watching a movie with explicit scenes of sex on a smartphone. What do you do?
   a. Report the matter to the substitute teacher upon his/her return to the classroom.
   b. Ignore what your friends are doing.
   c. Watch the movie with them; it is fun.
   d. Do your schoolwork.

7. Mrs. Brown, the Science teacher, left her iPad on her desk. You looked up just as Tyrone, the smartest boy in the class, moved it and hid it on the bookshelf. What do you do?
   a. Pretend you did not see what Tyrone did.
   b. Tell Mrs. Brown upon her return to the classroom.
   c. Get the iPad and secure it until Mrs. Brown returns.
   d. Tell Tyrone to put it back immediately.
   e. b, c, and d

8. Samantha has posted on Facebook some of the conversations she and her former friend Lisa shared. What should Lisa do?
   a. Post on Facebook some of the things Samantha wrote.
   b. Ignore Samantha's postings.
   c. Approach Samantha about her postings.
   d. Tell her parents or her Guidance Counselor.

9. Bradley is jealous that his ex-girlfriend, Brenda, is dating Jason now. He has texted Jason a threatening message about fighting him after school. What should Jason do?
   a. Get his boys together for the fight after school.
   b. Tell his Guidance Counselor, an administrator or a teacher.
   c. Ignore Bradley.
   d. End the relationship with Brenda.

10. Your best friend, Julie, lied to her mom telling her she has one Facebook account. However, your friend has another Facebook account where she communicates with her 30-year old Jitney driver boyfriend. What do you do?
    a. Tell Julie's mom about the second Facebook account.
    b. Tell Julie to close the account and discontinue seeing the Jitney driver.
    c. Ignore what Julie is doing; it is none of your business.
    d. Either A or B.

Fort Montague – Nassau, Bahamas

"Protect yourself - you are responsible for your actions." C.D. Minnis

Answer key for "How do you react?"

1. c, 2. d, 3. a, 4. d, 5. a, 6. a, 7. e, 8. d, 9. b, 10. d

I acknowledge my child has successfully completed chapter 9.

_____   _____

Parent/Guardian's Signature   Date

Chapter 10
Money Management

Letter to Parent/Guardian

Dear Parent/Guardian,

We are starting chapter 10 on _____ (Date).

In this chapter, we will learn the importance of saving. Additionally, by the end of this section, your child will also learn about being involved in a club/organization and giving of his/her time and talent to assist other individuals.

The following guest speakers will be invited:
1. Someone from a civic group to speak on, *"Helping the less fortunate in your Community."*
2. A representative from a bank or credit union who will give students tips on saving.

Warmest regards,

_____
Guidance Counselor/Teacher

BONDING ACTIVITY

Assist your child with developing good saving habits by each of you saving a dollar a day.

Deuteronomy 28:12 – "The Lord will open for you His good storehouse, the heavens, to give rain to your land in its season and to bless all the work of your hand; and you shall lend to many nations, but you shall not borrow."

You should learn about money at an early age. Learning about money includes saving, spending, donating and investing. Along with being taught how to save, you will also learn about sacrificing, giving up and doing without to get some of the things you want. Having saved to purchase your iPhone, you will appreciate it more.

Also, you need to understand the importance of smart spending. You don't buy an item just because you want it. You weigh how necessary the item is. Do you honestly need another tablet? Do you need another phone? According to the January – June 2016 edition of *The Bahamas Investor,* "There is a terribly low household savings rate in The Bahamas."

If you don't already have a savings account, ask your mummy, daddy, older sister or older brother to take you to the bank to open a bank account. Then when you have accumulated some money in your piggy bank, ask them to take you to the bank to put it in your savings account.

Instructions: Students will practice filling out deposit slips and balancing saving accounts.

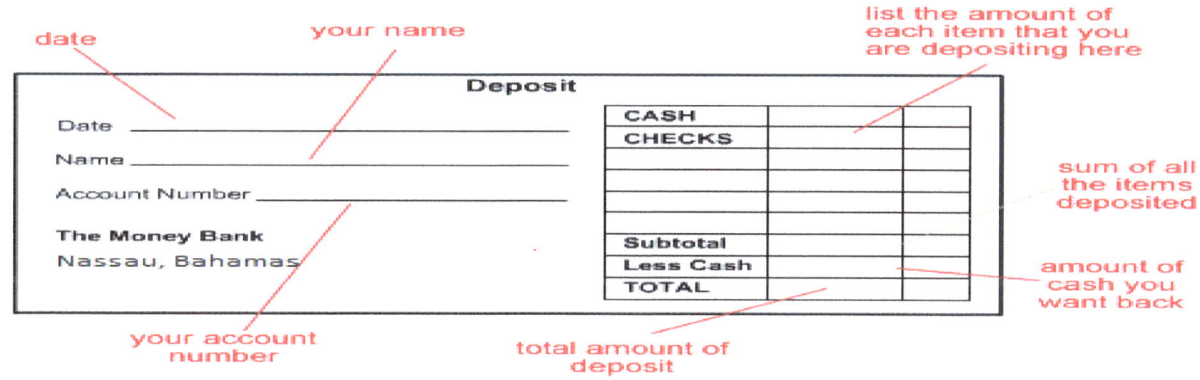

YOU CAN SAVE MORE

$1.00 a day for 365 days = a WHOPPING $365.00 for one year.

20___	January	February	March	April	May	June	July	August	September	October	November	December
1												
2												
3												
4												
5												
6												
7												
8												
9												
10												
11												
12												
13												
14												
15												
16												
17												
18												
19												
20												
21												
22												
23												
24												
25												
26												
27												
28												
29												
30												
31												
Total												

Proverbs 22:9 – "He who is generous will be blessed, for he gives some of his food to the poor."

You will appreciate it is not always about you and your needs. It is alright to:
- Give to others.
- Donate to charity.
- Share your lunch with your classmate who does not have any lunch.
- Give the less fortunate boy the pair of tennis shoes that have gotten too small for you.

It is essential you learn to save some of your money. However, not only should you be concerned about saving, but you should also use your time, talent and treasure for the benefit of others.

TIME TALENT TREASURE

How do you use your time, talent and treasure? You can use them to:
- ❖ Volunteer and help the less fortunate.
- ❖ Join your school's band, Governor General Youth Award (GGYA) or the Technical Cadet Corps Program (TCCP), etc.

Get involved. Students who are a member of a club/organization, perform better in school than their friends who are idle. As a member of a club or organization, you give of your time by attending the meetings and events planned by the club. You give of your talent by helping to sell goods, decorating or writing something for the club. You give of your treasure by donating your money to the club when paying dues or helping with a fundraising event.

> **Instructions: Students will create a survey/questionnaire on "T*he Importance of Community Service.*" Students will create bookmarks for an organization of their choice and sell them. Funds raised will be donated to the organization. Students will then generate a list of places where they can perform Community Service.**

Sponging
Red Bays, Andros
"Use your time and talent wisely." *C.D. Minnis*

I acknowledge my child has successfully completed chapter 10.

_____   _____

Parent/Guardian's Signature   Date

Chapter 11
Parental Involvement

Letter to Parent/Guardian

Dear Parent/Guardian,

    We are starting chapter 11 on _____ (Date).

    This chapter seeks to encourage you to become fully involved in the success of your child. Additionally, this section will focus on how you should monitor your child's use of the internet and how you can foster a better relationship with your child.

Warmest regards,

_____
Guidance Counselor/Teacher

BONDING ACTIVITY

Together with your child, create a list of activities you can do to foster a better relationship.

1. _____
2. _____
3. _____
4. _____
5. _____
6. _____

Proverbs 22:6 – "Train up a child in the way he should go, and even when he is old, he will not depart from it."

PARENTAL SUPPORT

Your child needs your help transitioning into Senior High School. Your child has been in the same Junior High School with the same friends for at least three years. This transitional period could be a most difficult time, but with your help, parents, this could happen quickly and without incident.

TIPS FOR PARENTS

1. Spend quality time with your child – go to the mall, to the beach together, take him/her shopping.
2. Know the administrators, guidance counselor, and teachers – get email addresses and phone contacts.
3. Know your child's friends – get the names of parents and phone contacts.
4. Check your child's books – go over classwork and homework.
5. Attend and participate in general Parents Teachers Association (PTA) Meetings and Grade Level Meetings.
6. Get a copy of the school's calendar to keep abreast of what's happening at your child's school, e.g., Midterm breaks, Report Card days.
7. Encourage your child to be respectful to administrators, teachers and fellow students.
8. Encourage your child to follow the rules of the school and society.
9. Get a tutor if your child is experiencing challenges in any subject.
10. Spend quality time with your child – go to the movies, go for lunch with your child, cook/bake together.

MONITOR YOUR CHILD'S USE OF THE INTERNET AND CELL PHONES

The internet is vital in today's society. Businesses can have their physical building in one country while operating their back office in another country. However, parents need to teach their children how to use the internet responsibly. Let your child know you will be monitoring his/her use of the web often. Tell him/her that he/she will have absolutely no privacy when it comes to the internet. You will need to know who he/she is communicating with on the web. He/she must give you every password he/she uses, or you will create one for him/her for all his/her internet accounts.

The following should help you keep some degree of knowledge about your child's internet use:

1. Password protect your home computer so you can monitor the amount of time your child spends on the web – Do not use passwords like:
    a. Your date of birth, b. Your mother's name, c. Your middle name.
2. When creating a password try to mix letters with numbers and symbols; this makes it very challenging for your child to figure out your password.
3. Check your computer's internet history regularly to see which sites your child has been visiting and if they're instant messaging.
4. Let your child know you're monitoring their email and messaging accounts to see who they're talking to on the internet.
5. After initial arguments with your child, he/she will understand, and it should help to prevent accusations of snooping later on.

Talk to your child about the possible dangers of chatting with strangers online, protecting their private information, and never sharing their password information with friends.

Parents, always keep the computer in the family room so you can monitor your child's use of the computer. Limit the amount of screen time they spend on the computer. Never allow your child to have a computer in his/her room.

Children use many terms when texting. Parents, here are some terms that your child may use when texting:

1. POS – parent over shoulder
2. BOL – be on later
3. WAY – where you at
4. ETC – everything cool
5. LMIRL – let's meet in real life
6. PAL – parents are listening
7. LMBO – laughing my butt off
8. HMU – hit me up
9. CD9 – code 9, parents around
10. "Slay" – doing something very well
11. 53X – sneaky way to type sex
12. KML – killing myself laughing
13. SMT – suck my teeth
14. IWSN – I want sex now
15. FWB – friends with benefit
16. IKR – I know right
17. OMG – Oh my God
18. LOL – laugh out loud
19. "Lit" – something awesome
20. "Trapsy" - troublesome

PARENTS BEWARE OF DRUGS AND YOUR CHILD

1. Students drink more at social events and home and as young as age 11.3 years.
2. Students purchase their cigarettes from stores.
3. 28.2% of all 12th grade male students have used marijuana, and they get marijuana from their friends. They start using marijuana as young as age 11.8 years.
4. Below are some of the household substances students use as solvents or inhalants:
    a. Cough medicine
    b. Deodorants
    c. Gasoline
    d. Glues
    e. Inhalants:
        i. Nail polish remover
        ii. Felt-tip marker fluids
        iii. Cooking sprays

Courtesy of *"The Bahamas Secondary School Drug Prevalence Survey 2012"* by National Anti-Drug Secretariat, The Bahamas National Drug Council

Students who are exposed to alcohol and drugs because their parents drink and use drugs are more likely to drink and use drugs. Parents, you must be a living example for your child.

HANDS-ON PARENTAL INVOLVEMENT

1. Show your child love – give him/her hugs and kisses regularly.
2. Always listen to him/her, even when it seems like he/she is not making any sense.
3. Speak positively into his/her spirit.
4. Your child needs your explicit support; attend any extracurricular activities they are involved in, e.g., their sporting events.
5. Assure him/her that you are his/her number one fan.
6. Show your child love – encourage him/her to have an "*I can do it*" attitude.

PARENT'S PLEDGE

1. I will **HELP** my child to graduate as an Honor Roll student.
2. I will **TEACH** my child to be respectful to administrators, staff and fellow students.
3. I will **INSTRUCT** my child to obey the school's rules
4. I will **GUARANTEE** my child attends school properly dressed each day.
5. I will **ENSURE** my child has all the necessary materials for every class each day.
6. I will **ENCOURAGE** my child to have a positive attitude.
7. I will **FOSTER** an "I can" attitude in my child.
8. I will **TEACH** my child how to say, *"please," "thank you," "pardon me," "excuse me," "may I," "yes sir," "no sir," "yes ma'am," "no ma'am,"* etc.
9. I will **ENSURE** my child comes to school in good health each day.
10. I will **PRAISE** my child when he/she does well and **ENCOURAGE** him/her when he/she is challenged.

WHAT I LEARNED ...

Congratulations! I commend you for completing *Transitioning into Senior High School.* You are now equipped with skills that will help you develop into a well-rounded individual. You will succeed. You will be an 'A' student at your new school. Use the space below to write one thought that you will remember about each chapter of the book, and how it can help you become the successful person you are capable of becoming.

Chapter 1...Welcome to Senior High School _____

_____

Chapter 2.....Grade 10-Results Oriented _____

_____

Chapter 3.....Your Guidance Counselor _____

_____

Chapter 4.....Graduation Requirements _____

_____

Chapter 5.....Study Skills _____

_____

Chapter 6.....Your Future is in Your Hands _____

_____

Chapter 7.....Healthy Living _____

_____

Chapter 8......Drug Awareness _____

_____

Chapter 9....Proper Use of the Internet, Social Media & Cell Phones_____

_____

Chapter 10.....Money Management _____

_____

Chapter 11....Parental Involvement _____

APPENDIX A
STUDENT PROGRESS REPORT

SCHOOL: _____ DATE: _____
STUDENT: _____ GRADE: _____

Your child is a capable student who has lots of ability. To ensure your child realizes his/her full potential, have your child's teachers complete this form, and return it to you so you can monitor your child's progress in school. Have this Student Progress Report form completed once monthly.

SUBJECTS	GRADES TO DATE	TEACHER	COMMENTS	TEACHER'S SIGNATURE
English Language				
English Literature				
Mathematics				
Biology				
Physical Education				
Civics				
Religion				
History				
Geography				
_____				
_____				
_____				
_____				

PLEASE SELECT THE APPROPRIATE COMMENT(S):			
1	Student worked well	9	Student was disruptive
2	Student was punctual	10	Excessive talking
3	Student behaved well	11	Student is tardy
4	Has all school supplies	12	Refuses to cooperate
5	Complete assignments	13	Disrespectful
6	Cooperative, respectful	14	Parent Conference needed
7	Student's work has improved	15	Needs continual guidance
8	Behavior is improving		

APPENDIX B
EMERGENCY CONTACT NUMBERS
CALL ANY ONE OF THE FOLLOWING AGENCIES FOR HELP:

AGENCIES	PHONE	PHONE	PHONE
ADOLESCENT HEALTH SERVICES	328-3248/9		
AIDS SECRETARIAT	328-2260	323-5968	325-2281
ALCOHOLIC ANONYMOUS	322-1685		
BAHAMAS NATIONAL DRUG COUNCIL	325-4633/4	326-5355	326-5340
CHILD ABUSE HOTLINE (GRAND BAHAMA)	351-7763		
CHILD ABUSE HOTLINE (NEW PROVIDENCE)	322-2763	422-2763	
CHILD PROTECTION SERVICES	397-2550		
CHRISTIAN COUNSELING CENTER	323-7000		
COMMUNITY COUNSELING & ASSESSMENT CENTER	323-3293		
COMMUNITY MENTAL HEALTH	323-3295/9		
CRIMINAL INVESTIGATIVE UNIT	322-2561	322-2562	
CRISIS CENTER (GRAND BAHAMA)	352-4357		
CRISIS CENTER (NEW PROVIDENCE)	328-0922	322-4999	
DEPARTMENT OF SOCIAL SERVICES	397-2524		
DOMESTIC VIOLENCE	323-0171	323-3859	
DRUG ENFORCEMENT UNIT	323-7139	323-7140	
HEALTH SOCIAL SERVICES – FAMILY VIOLENCE	356-3350	356-4468	
NATIONAL HOTLINE	322-2763	422-2763	
NATIONAL LEAD INSTITUTE	328-5323	525-3749	698-6384
NORTHEASTERN ALLIANCE SUSPENSION PROGRAM	356-3103/5	356-2158	
PACE SCHOOL	356-0943		
POLICE	911	919	
POLICE VICTIM SUPPORT	328-5670		
PUBLIC HEALTH DEPARTMENT	502-4700	322-8835	
SANDILANDS REHABILITATION CENTER	364-9600		
SCHOOL PSYCHOLOGICAL SERVICES	502-2948		
SURE	341-2949		
SUSPECTED CHILD ABUSE AND NEGLECT UNIT (SCAN)	322-5823	323-8438	
T.A.P.S.	393-0706	393-0672	394-3064

APPENDIX C

School Supplies

- Pencil pouch
- Blue or black pens
- No. 2 pencils
- Pencil sharpener
- Highlighters
- Permanent markers
- Erasers
- Three-ring binders
- Three-hole punch
- Loose-leaf paper
- Black & White notebooks
- Graph paper
- Folders
- Glue
- Post-its
- Wite-Out
- Protractor
- Ruler
- Scissors
- Graphing calculator
- Book bag
- P.E. Kit
- Hand sanitizers
- Textbooks required by the school

Minnis / Secondary School / 75

APPENDIX D

STUDENT INFORMATION SHEET

Your Guidance Counselor is here to assist you. Please complete this form and return it to your counselor at the beginning of the term.

NAME OF STUDENT: _____

DATE OF BIRTH: _____

JUNIOR HIGH SCHOOL: _____

HOMEROOM CLASS: _____ HOMEROOM TEACHER: _____

MOTHER'S NAME: _____

PHONE (H)_____ (C)_____ (W)_____

FATHER'S NAME: _____

PHONE (H)_____ (C)_____ (W)_____

STUDENT LIVES WITH: _____

PHONE (H)_____ (C)_____ (W)_____

PATHWAY: _____ SOCIAL SCIENCE: _____

[PHOTO]

Do you have any medical/emotional problems that have been medically diagnosed and may affect you during the course of the day? E.g., Asthmatic, depression, heart condition: ☐ YES   ☐ NO

If yes, please list medical/emotional problems: _____

Medication(s) being used: _____

Do you have any known allergies?   ☐ YES   ☐ NO

If yes, please list allergies: _____

Medication(s) being used: _____

B.J.C. PASSES:

SUBJECTS	GRADE	SUBJECTS	GRADE

YOUR INTEREST/TALENT

Please place a tick next to the item(s) you are good at:

Artist: ☐ painting ☐ drawing ☐ craft
Agriculture: ☐ growing things (fruits & vegetables and/or flowers)
Athlete: ☐ track and field ☐ basketball ☐ soccer ☐ swimming ☐ volleyball Other _____
☐ Building things from wood ☐ drawing a house plan
☐ Cooking ☐ baking
Computer: ☐ creating videos ☐ repairing the computer ☐ graphics Other _____
Electronics: ☐ repairing clocks, television, computers, etc.
☐ Fixing hair ☐ barbering
Music: ☐ play an instrument ☐ sing ☐ write music ☐ dance Other _____
Writing: ☐ songs ☐ poetry
Any other interest/talent: _____

APPENDIX E

Parent/Guardian Consent Form
for Group Counseling

I, _____ (Parent's name) give permission for my child, _____ of grade _____ to participate in Group Counseling activities.

The Group Counseling will run from _____ to _____. The group is entitled _____. Some subjects to be covered in the group are as follows:

_____

_____

This group will be led by (Ms., Mrs. Mr.) _____ of the Guidance Department.

The group leader(s) will keep the information shared by group members confidential, except in situations where:

1. Any student reveals information about harm to himself/herself or any other person.
2. Any child discloses information about abuse or molestation.
3. Any child divulges information about criminal activity, or the court (a judge) subpoenas counseling records.

The counselor is mandated to report the information immediately to the relevant authority.

By signing this form, I give my informed consent for my child to participate in Group Counseling.

Please print parent/guardian's name _____

Signature of parent/guardian _____

Please print student's name _____

Signature of student _____

Date _____

APPENDIX F

Parent/Guardian Consent Form
for Individual Counseling

I give permission for the Guidance Counselor, (Ms., Mrs., Mr.) _____ to conduct Individual Counseling with my child, _____ of grade _____.

The Individual Counseling sessions will run from _____ to _____.

The relationship between counselor and client relies on trust. The counselor will keep the information shared by the student confidential, except in situations where the counselor is obligated to report the information to the relevant authority. The following information must be reported immediately:

1. The student reveals information about harm to himself or any other person.
2. The child discloses information about abuse or molestation.
3. The child divulges information about criminal activity, or the court (a judge) subpoenas counseling records.

By signing this form, I give my informed consent for my child to participate in Individual Counseling.

Please print parent/guardian's name _____

Signature of parent/guardian _____

Please print student's name _____

Signature of student _____

Date _____

APPENDIX G
CERTIFICATE OF COMPLETION

School _____

CERTIFICATE OF COMPLETION

This certificate is presented to

_____

Congratulations! You have successfully completed *Transitioning Into Senior High School.*

_____ _____
Guidance Counselor/Teacher *Parent/Guardian*

Date: _____

REFERENCES

The Champion's Ride by Allison Manswell
How To Get Good Grades by Lee County Public Schools
The 7 Habits of Highly Effective Teens by Sean Covey
Bahamas Secondary School Drug Prevalence Survey 2012 by National Anti-Drug Secretariat, The Bahamas National Drug Council
Positive Classroom Management by Terri Breeden & Emalie Egan
The Bahamas National Drug Council
The American Council for Drugs
www.cob.edu.bs
www.btvi.org.bs
www.bamsibahamas.com
Cyberbullying: New problems, new tactics. www.kidshealth.org
Information Security Services. www.tevora.com
www.WikiHowtodoanything
Photos courtesy of:
1. www.abacobahamas.com
2. www.theworldtraveler.com

The Bahamas Investor January – June 2016 edition

MEET THE AUTHOR

Carol D. Minnis worked as a classroom teacher for fifteen (15) years and as a Guidance Counselor for fourteen (14) years. She started her teaching career at Hawksbill High School in Grand Bahama, then moved to Central Andros High School, her alma mater. She later served at L.W. Young Junior/Senior High School, Doris Johnson Senior High School, C.V. Bethel Senior High School, C.I. Gibson Senior High School and is currently posted at the Transitional Alternative Program for Students (T.A.P.S.). Ms. Minnis has interacted with students from all strata of society.

Ms. Minnis completed her graduate studies at Kent State University in collaboration with the now, University of The Bahamas, obtaining a Masters of Education in School Counseling. Her Bachelor of Science degree is in Secondary Education from Fort Valley State University, Fort Valley, Georgia. She obtained her high school education at Central Andros High School, Andros, Bahamas.

Ms. Minnis is presently serving as a Guidance Counselor and is employed by the Ministry of Education. As department head and grade level counselor, she worked tirelessly implementing programs to help students realize their full potential. She enjoys working with teenagers and gets much joy out of helping them become responsible and productive citizens.

She is a member of Holy Cross Anglican Church where she serves as an usher. Her favorite scripture verses are Romans 8:28, *"For all things work together for good to those who love The Lord, for those who are called according to His purpose."* Ephesians 3:20 *"Now unto Him, that can do **exceedingly**, **abundantly above all that we ask** or **think**, or **imagine.**"*

Her hobbies include traveling, reading and gardening.

Working on a Family Island comes with its challenges. Working in the school system demands much of us as individuals. Working on the island of San Salvador as the only counselor for both the primary school and the senior high school is a mammoth task. It is with pleasure I embrace ***Transitioning into Senior High School*** written by Carol D. Minnis. I am convinced this book will undoubtedly make the delivery of counseling to my students more effective. I am delighted the content of this book is Bahamian based, and my students will be able to identify with the material.

Transitioning into Senior High School is an interactive book that will serve as a valuable tool for my students as they prepare for life after high school. Also, I am sure my students' parents will treasure this book as it has many bonding activities that will afford them countless opportunities to bond with their child and form a closer relationship.

I highly recommend the use of ***Transitioning into Senior High School*** in all schools throughout the Commonwealth of The Bahamas.

    Sandra Gay-Morley
    Guidance Counselor
    United Estates Primary School & San Salvador Central High School

---

My daughter will be entering grade 10 at a private school for the first time in September. As a single parent, I am delighted to see a book of this nature, which should make transitioning for her from a government school to a private school as a 10th grade student easier.

I love the entire book. However, the bonding activities at the beginning of each chapter will keep me abreast of what my daughter is doing and more actively involved in her learning process. I am confident chapter 11, "Parental Involvement" will be a section I refer to throughout her high school years, and not just while she is in grade 10.

I recommend ***Transitioning into Senior High School*** to every parent, as I am certain it will make a positive difference in their life and the life of their child.

    Doneka Braithwaite, Parent

Transitioning into Senior High School is a Bahamian book that will be beneficial to every child in senior high schools throughout the Commonwealth of the Bahamas. It depicts pictures from various islands:

1. *Columbus Landing,* San Salvador
2. *Salt Ponds,* Inagua
3. *Androsia Batik,* Andros
4. *Sir Sidney Poitier Bridge,* Nassau
5. *Fort Montague,* Nassau
6. *Sponging,* Andros

This is an interactive resource book that should alleviate the fears of both parent and child as the child begins senior high school. Also, the counselor will appreciate this book as it will make delivery of the counseling sessions lively and provocative in the high school setting.

www.ingramcontent.com/pod-product-compliance
Lightning Source LLC
Chambersburg PA
CBHW042013150426
43196CB00002B/30